Twin Sisters

Based on real characters

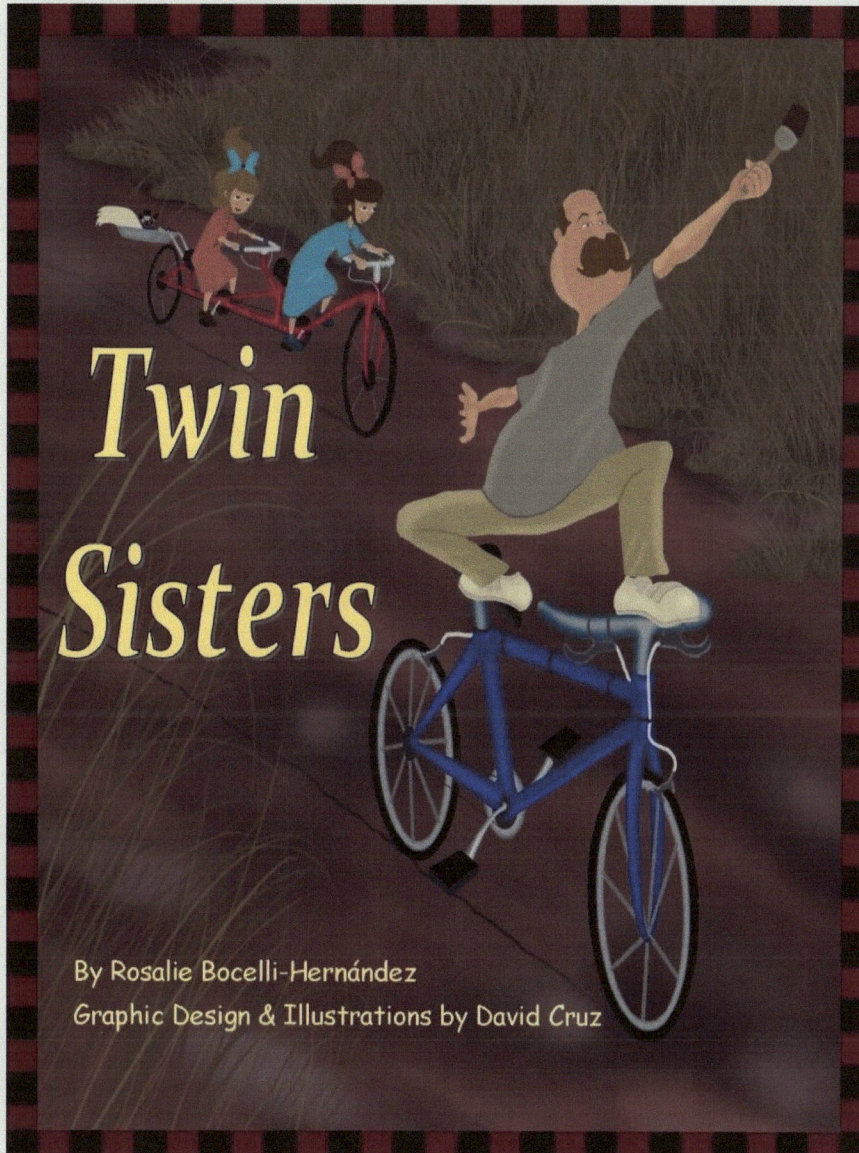

I0144137

Twin Sisters

By Rosalie Bocelli-Hernández

Graphic Design & Illustrations by David Cruz

English version

Revised: August 2017

Copyrights © 2014 Rosalie Bocelli-Hernández
Graphic Design & Illustrator David Cruz
ISBN 978-0-9908444-1-9
Story Translated by Carlos Ian Cuevas
Edited by Margaret A. Jordan

Dedication

I dedicate this book to our Lord God, He gave me the opportunity to publish this story based on real people; to my husband Carlos for being there for me all these years; to my lovely sons: Carlos Daniel and Gabriel Sebastian, I dedicate this book to my cousin-brother, David Cruz who was the instrument of God and did the illustration in this book and encouraged me to publish it;

I also dedicate it to Devin and Trajen Womack, two brothers full of talents and grace of God.

To my sister and brother Lourdes G. Rodríguez and Miguel A. Rodríguez for their support and love.

To Dr. Larry Woods who one day came to my office and with his words inspired me to publish this story; and to the protagonists: Cristina and Milagros for allowing me to publish their legacy and for being the source of my inspiration.

Chapter 1

Every morning I would look at my grandfather as he got on his bicycle and pedaled out to the prairie, looking for a view that would strike his fancy. He was very keen on finding the right light, especially those early rays. At night, he would wait for the moon to rise among the stars until it would reflect in the stream as if in a mirror. Painting nature, feeling as if he was part of nature, was my Grandpa Felix's main joy.

One afternoon grandpa Félix told me:

— "Milagros, I'd like you and your sister, Cristina to help me paint these beautiful landscapes that are part of our Puerto Rico." He looked into my eyes and continued, "It is time to work on your talents."

My grandpa Félix was a strong and determined man. He was full of energy and had a gift for drawing and painting. I immediately went looking for my sister to give her the great news. When I found her, I could barely contain my excitement. "Cristina, grandpa said he would teach us how to paint!"

I knew this would over joy my sister, since she had been fascinated by drawings and paintings from an early age. Her face lit up and her smile was reflected in her big brown eyes.

- "Grandpa said that?"

- "Yes!"

Chapter 2

Cristina and I were twins but not identical.
Cristina looked more like our mama while I
resembled my aunt Carlota.

The day of our birth was a very happy one for
our parents. The doctor and nurses in the delivery
room had been delighted to discover that we were
healthy twin girls.

Dad was born in the Dominican Republic; one of
the Greater Antilles islands in the Caribbean Sea.
Dad met my mama in one of his trips to Puerto Rico.
His kindness and chivalry conquered her heart, and
a few years later they were married.

My mother was admired by many people,

especially by her children. She was a beautiful woman with piercing green eyes. Her intelligence and artistic talents were expressed through her designs and haute couture.

Chapter 3

Grandpa Félix would look for a perfect view every single morning. Then, in the afternoon, we would follow him on our tandem bicycle, the book bag filled with paints, brushes, and sketchbooks. Grandpa taught us how to feel nature as it breathed, and how to see details we had never known were there.

He taught us how to observe the morning dew on the leaves, the spouting of flowers along the green meadow, the stillness of the lake and the sound of the rolling river. To contemplate the light as it fell over the leaves and radiated shades of green, yellow, and brown.

I started to feel as if I was part of nature itself. Later on, I would understand that what I was experiencing came from God: "Man was created from the dust of the ground and to dust he would return." The most important thing in life was the way your soul felt when you were in contact with nature and your Creator.

One afternoon I made a net out of paper and ran across the meadow, trying to capture a butterfly of sublime beauty. Its wings were black, green, orange and purple. At the very tip they were blue, as deep as the deepest reaches of the sea. It was big and lovely. I was enthralled and followed it over hills and valleys with my net.

After many attempts, I was able to catch it. I grabbed it gently with my fingers and touched its soft wings. I noticed that, for a brief moment, it had stayed still. I looked at it and said — "Pretty butterfly, I just want to make a drawing of you, please be calm." And I think it understood me, since it didn't try to fly away.

Before I let it go I brought it close to my face, so I could say goodbye. Its silky wings caressed my cheeks. I kissed it tenderly and said, "Goodbye, my friend," and let it fly off.

At that moment I heard grandpa's voice, calling me: "Milagros! Milagros!" I ran in the direction of his voice. When I found him, he said, "Let me see what you drew today!" Grandpa examined my drawing carefully. There was something there he couldn't quite make out at first, but of course, I could. I had drawn the butterfly with the face of my sister Cristina. I had felt, somehow, that the butterfly and I belonged together, same as my sister and me.

From the seeds of love of my parents we were born: Cristina and Milagros, twin sisters. It was as if we shared the same feelings, the same heart. We loved being together. It was a thing of beauty.

Chapter 4

When my sister and I became young adults, we worked in the areas of sewing, drawing, and graphic design at the Carlota Alfaro building. This building carries the name of our aunt, Carlota Alfaro, and it is located in Santurce, Puerto Rico. My mom, my sister and I worked there for many years. The fashion designs of my aunt and my mother have been recognized all over the world, from Europe and the United States to Latin America.

Grandpa Félix was right when he said that Cristina and I had many talents. Today I feel very

proud of my grandpa Félix, my mother, and my aunt, for teaching us to appreciate the arts. This was a big lesson for me, one that I decided to pass on to my daughter, Misscha Liz. I began to put her in contact with the arts when she was two and a half years old.

As I grew older I learned to believe in myself, and especially to value other people in my life. I am proud of myself and of my sister Cristina for the talent God bestowed upon us… just two more of His faithful creatures, and twin sisters.

Questions:

1. What is the title of the story?

2. Who are the characters?

3. Who narrates the story?

4. What do you most like of the story?

5. What do you think is the message of the author?

6. What did you learn from the story?

7. What would you like to do when you grow up?

8. Do you have any skill or talent?

   - Draw?

   - Paint?

   - Sing?

- Recite poetry?

9. Do you play any musical instrument?

10. Which one?

11. Do you practice a sport?

12. Which one?

13. Any other talent or skill that we haven't mentioned?

14. Describe your talents; please tell me more about them?

10. After reading this story, what you are going to do with your talents?

Author's Note:
Please write to the author with your comments about the story and how you will use your talents from now on?
Send your thoughts to: basedonrealstory@gmail.com

27

Glossary:

Art- *skill; talent: draw, sing, paint, or play an instrument*

Gentlemanliness –*polite person, noble, educated*

Capture – *grab, hunt, hold up*

Dressmaker – *person that sews a dress or any dress clothes such as pants, shirt, skirt, curtain and so on.*

Deposited – *he gave, gave*

Graphic Design – *drawing on paper or computer*

Tandem bicycle – *a bicycle with two seats*

Scenario – *view, panorama*

Sky – *sky infinity*

Twins –*one of two children born from the same parent and the same day birth; their faces are very similar or identical.*

Germinate – *formed, grow, flourish, bloom*

Defenseless – *weak, helpless, unable to move*

Landscape – *panorama view*

Prairie – *pasture, grassland, countryside,*

Net - *sieve, paper strainer*

Revealed – *discovered, explained, taught*

Creek – *little river*

Morning dew – *water drops deposited on leaves, grass, trees and flowers in the morning*

Sublime beauty – *beautiful, spiritual thing*

Talent – *capacity, gift of God*

Book bag, back pack, suitcase

Draw

Draw any thing that you liked from the story.

Important Note: *This story is available in English, Spanish in print, and e-book.*

New books published in 2016

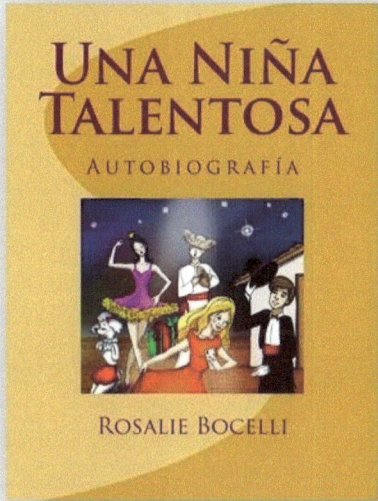

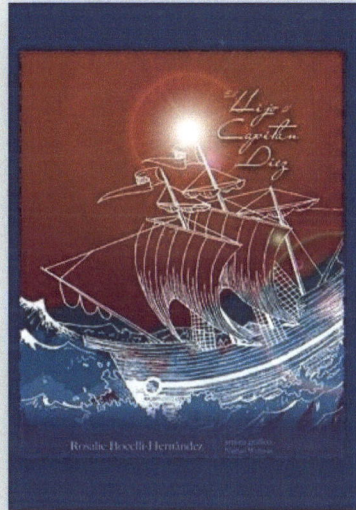

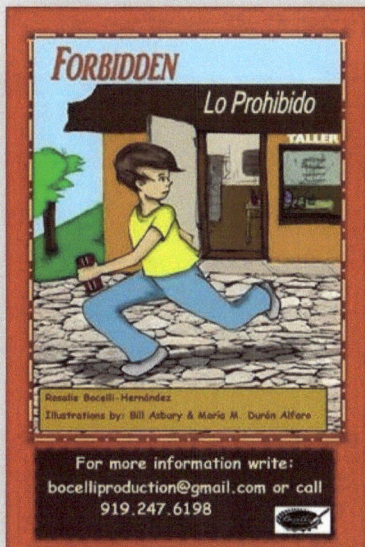

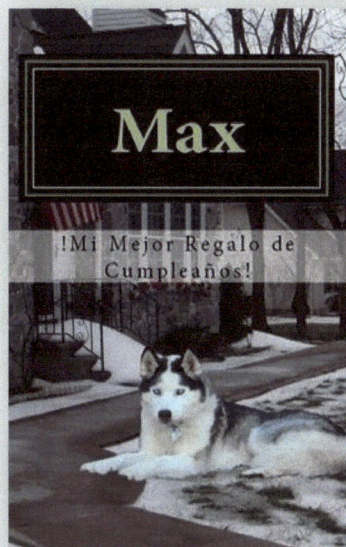

UNA NIÑA TALENTOSA
AUTOBIOGRAFÍA
ROSALIE BOCELLI

Rosalie Bocelli-Hernández

FORBIDDEN
Lo Prohibido
TALLER

Rosalie Bocelli-Hernández
Illustrations by: Bill Asbury & Maria M. Durán Alfaro

For more information write:
bocelliproduction@gmail.com or call
919.247.6198

Max
¡Mi Mejor Regalo de Cumpleaños!

Author's Biography

Rosalie was born in the picturesque island of Puerto Rico. She started to be exposed in the dramatic arts, since she was three years old. Her first performance was in the Classic Drama of Snow White. At the age of 16th her history class teacher challenged students to do a presentation based on the Greek literature of Homer's, The Iliad. Rosalie wrote her first script based on this novel. The play was so successful that her teacher gave four A's for her excellent performance and screenplay. A few months later a group from her church invited her to be part of a group of writers who produced children's stories for a Christian Radio Program.

In 1996, Kodak Eastman offered Rosalie a job in RTP North Carolina where she moved with her family. A few years after she started to co-host a TV show on a Time Warner Station. In 2014, Rosalie published her first children's book based on real characters title: Twin Sisters and in January 2016 she published: "Una Niña Talentosa". This is a biography based on her.

Rosalie completed her Master Degree in 2015 and starting her doctorate in Education at Southeastern Baptist Theological Seminary in Wake Forest, in 2016. She works at Durham Parks and Recreation, planning, developing, and coordinating events and programs for the Latino Community. She has been sharing her personal and professional experience in helping the community. She enjoys producing professional and quality work in order to help Latinos and the community as a whole. God has been blessing her with a wonderful husband, Carlos Hernández and two sons: Gabriel Sebastian and Carlos Daniel Hernández.

www.ingramcontent.com/pod-product-compliance
Lightning Source LLC
Chambersburg PA
CBHW041222040426
42443CB00002B/54